W9-BIA-745

Published by The Child's World®
1980 Lookout Drive • Mankato, MN 56003-1705
800-599-READ • www.childsworld.com

ACKNOWLEDGMENTS
The Child's World®: Mary Berendes, Publishing Director
The Design Lab: Design and page production
Red Line Editorial: Editorial direction

LIBRARY OF CONGRESS CATALOGING-IN-PUBLICATION DATA
Heinrichs, Ann.
  Prepositions / by Ann Heinrichs ; illustrated by Dan McGeehan and
David Moore.
     p. cm.
  Includes bibliographical references and index.
  ISBN 978-1-60253-431-5 (library bound : alk. paper)
  1. English language—Prepositions—Juvenile literature. I. McGeehan,
Dan, ill. II. Moore, David, ill. III. Title.
  PE1335.H443 2010
  428.2—dc22   2010011460

Printed in the United States of America in Mankato, Minnesota.
July 2010
F11538

ABOUT THE AUTHOR

Ann Heinrichs was lucky. Every year from grade three through grade eight, she had a big, fat grammar textbook and a grammar workbook. She feels that this prepared her for life. She is now the author of more than 100 books for children and young adults. She has also enjoyed successful careers as a children's book editor and an advertising copywriter. Ann grew up in Fort Smith, Arkansas, and lives in Chicago, Illinois.

ABOUT THE ILLUSTRATORS

Dan McGeehan spent his younger years as an actor, author, playwright, cartoonist, editor, and even as a casket maker. Now he spends his days drawing little monsters!

David Moore is an illustration instructor at a university who loves painting and flying airplanes. Watching his youngest daughter draw inspires David to illustrate children's books.

On

TABLE OF CONTENTS

What Is a Preposition?   4

It Never Stands Alone   12

At the Beginning   14

One Will Do   16

According to Me   20

Lots of Prepositions!   22

How to Learn More   23

Glossary   24

Index   24

What Is a Preposition?

In the morning, Skipper runs
between the rows of apple trees
along the edge of the park.

All the red words in this sentence are **prepositions**.
They **connect** words with one another. Many
prepositions are short words—in, on, of, at, and by.
Others are much longer, such as between, outside,
underneath, and throughout.

What would you do without prepositions? You'd have trouble saying anything at all! Prepositions can point out a time.

on Tuesday

in July

at noon

by three o'clock

around midnight

between classes

I like snacks around midnight.

Prepositions can point out a place.

on the chair

in school

at the library

by the benches

around the corner

between your eyes

Or, they can help describe something.

the monster with the blue nose

books for class

a longhorn steer from Texas

11

It Never Stands Alone

Put the hamster's cage behind the *couch.*

This story was written about *me.*

This trophy belongs to *her.*

I've been confused until *now.*

A preposition never stands alone. It is always followed by the word or words it is linking to the rest of the sentence. This word or **phrase** is called the **object**. The orange words above are prepositions. The italic words are objects.

The object answers a question: Whom? Where? When?

At the Beginning

A preposition and its object can also go at the beginning of a sentence. When this phrase comes first, a **comma** (,) usually follows it.

In the *shadows*, a yellow bird appeared.

Across the *marsh*, we heard the sounds of croaking frogs.

At *sunset*, the guards lowered the flag.

From the bushes, the monster can see me!

One Will Do

The monster likes fish for breakfast and for lunch.

Some flowers grow in spring, in summer, and in fall.

Sometimes you don't have to repeat the preposition. These sentences work better if you remove the extra prepositions.

The monster likes fish for breakfast and lunch.

Some flowers grow in spring, summer, and fall.

17

Sometimes people use two prepositions in a row when one will do just fine.

The pie fell off ~~of~~ the windowsill.

The critter stayed inside ~~of~~ its cave.

According to Me

He was out of control.

I'll have peas instead of broccoli.

According to Bill, the party's over.

Sometimes several words act together as a preposition. In this case, you need all the words. Other examples are in addition to, in regard to, on account of, in spite of.

Lots of Prepositions!

A frog sits on a log in the reeds near the edge of the pond.

Sometimes it takes a lot of prepositions to say what you mean! The sentence above tells exactly where that frog is. How many prepositions can you use in a sentence?

I'm sitting on the mat with the fish in the dish.